A Late Recognition of the Signs
ERIKA BURKART

*Translated
from the German and
with an afterword by
Marc Vincenz*

SPUYTEN DUYVIL

New York City

Acknowledgements:

"The Shivers," "After Anesthesia, November 11, 2005" and "Getting Dark" were originally published in *MadHat 14*. "Erika Burkart: Fragments, Shards, and Visions" was previously published in Hyperion Journal.

Copyright ©2015 Ernst Halter
Translation copyright ©2015 by Marc Vincenz
ISBN 978-0-923389-10-9

Cover photo taken in the gardens of Haus Kapf,
Aargau (Erika Burkart and Ernst Halter's residence)
©2014 Marc Vincenz

Library of Congress Cataloging-in-Publication Data

Burkart, Erika, 1922-2010.
 [*Das späte Erkennen der Zeichen*. English]
 A late recognition of the signs / by Erika Burkart ;
Translated from the German by Marc Vincenz.
    pages cm
 "Originally published in German as *Das späte Erkennen der Zeichen*"
 ISBN 978-0-923389-10-9
 I. Vincenz, Marc, translator. II. Title.
 PT2662.U68E5613 2013
 831'.914--dc23

                                2013017447

A Late Recognition of the Signs

Contents

1
QUESTION AND COMPLAINT

Housekeeping 3
The Shivers 4
Winter-Sick 5
Old Woman in December 7
The Long Way 9
The Nursery 10
Posthumous 11
Understanding 12
White Rosebud 13
Looking Back 14
Forest Cemetery (after Mörike) 15
Estrangement 16
Question and Complaint 17
After Anesthesia, November 11, 2005
18
The Cold Night 20
Directions 21
The Stillness 22
Cast Out (Desert) 23
The Legendary Shepherds 24
Sheep in the Snow 25
Evening 27
Gras (Grass) 29

The Shadow   30
Morning Twilight   31
The Bridge   32

2
THE MESSAGE IN THE SNOWFLAKE

Path
Childhood in the Old House   38
Elective Affinity   40
Dark Hour   42
Pre-Pre-Spring   43
Alley   44
Magical Number   46
Night Bird   48
The Guest   49
The Coffin   50
Sea of Fog, as seen from Lindenberg   51
White Death   52
For Markus Manfred Jung   54
Fatigue in March   55
Waiting Room: The Protest   56
Forgotten Path   57
Harvest   58
Summer Solstice   59
Childhood Sun   60

About Waking from Dreams 62
Night-Thought 63
Moon in March 64
Reading Material 65
From the Cloud Nation 67
Vita 68
Mid-Winter Spring 69
Getting Dark 71
Key Word 73
Death and the Woman 74
Spring 75
The Message in the Snowflake 76

AFTERWORD

Erika Burkart:
Fragments, Shards, and Visions 79

"His voice, like
a bird's that only touched
sand in flight, full of desire
to end the resting
and move with the wind."
> —Martin Buber, *The Living Dead*

"Stay with us, for it is toward evening and the day is now far spent."
> —Luke 24:29 ESV

"A poem may be able to contain the echo of the storm
like that mussel touched
by Orpheus in flight."
> —Adam Zagajewski,
> from the poem, "Mussel"

1
Question and Complaint

Housekeeping

Bulb burnt out,
shoes dirty,
the day is short and light austere,
almost nothing remains
except mourning and seven books;
I will read them again one more time,
before the old eyes blur
into blackness—books,
I suspect, are unknown over there.

The Shivers

Where two dots blink,
two suns bedazzle—
that's already
the puzzle of the face;
you aren't it.
I am not it.
It's one of those demons
that flash out of cracks,
reside behind walls,
glare in the windows, they squat
to the right, skulk to the left—
I shudder
as if locked in a block of ice;
they call this freezing, which arises
between three and four in the night, the shivers.

There is a time
when one doesn't wait anymore,
denigrated to an alien
in the body-shivers.

The loyalty of foolish rhymes remains.
Little is permitted to rhyme in life
except words, which germinate
in the darkness of a poem.

Winter-Sick

This morning a large
black bird flew by the window—
no crow, but a messenger
swarmed
in life-feigning leaves.

How I dread the winter,
the frost and freezing,
the long-short, grim days,
that graphically aesthetic shadow-palette:
mandatory grey,
deathly white and leafless black
waving evergreen to me in the ice wind.

That was another time, when I loved
the colorless white, the open mirror.
Throwing off sparks, it shot and salvaged,
sucked in all the colors;
rainbow fragments,
how did they get on the wall?
Reflections were inexplicable to the child.
Eden was white
when in the night
the sky fell to earth—

in the mornings, snow that flew in secretly
tasted sacred
and still unscathed by tracks,
lost paths led far away,
for the light flowed
out of first light.

Old Woman in December

Far from her view of the world
the old woman concentrates
on her jacket:
it's happened again,
third button in the second hole—
and where's that handkerchief?
misplaced? lost?
People are not like they used to be,
can't trust anyone anymore.
They finagle. Test and amuse themselves.

Between 4 and 5 in late afternoon,
dim murkiness in the absence
of rising comfort,
she recalls
the night's eyes when she was a child—
huddling at the window in twilight,
the frosty, clear sky
with a pink, downy ground-cloud in the southeast.

Ice clouds; cold glow.
The old woman freezes, grasps her own right hand,
recalling tears released by warmth,
she doesn't turn on the light;
hermetic darkness dams in the window,
the stove spits sparks,
tiles still store radiation—
as it, an anonymous compassion,
shelters from the dread,
in that dead-cold
that petrifies body and soul.

The Long Way

The story is old
and the forest deep.
They slaughtered him.
Where do you now lock up
those bird-girls?
the outlawed
forest nymphs?
Even now they're still looking out
for that red flower.

There goes Joringel,
bent over the flower—
searching for the nightingale,
hears the toads—
the castle had sunk,
only a wild path remained
in the night forest
branching out to the furthest stars.

Those who miss each other
don't forget.

The Nursery

One hour apart
on the edge of a nursery,
fir trees launch
into their light green sprouting,
centaurium weed
blossoms behind the trellis,
moongrass nods in fans over stumps,
stalks harden their cutting edge
over mycelia and pale mushrooms;
moss swells, the mouse burrows, bones frighten,
the gnome eavesdrops under the roots.

On the other side of the moor, out of town,
along the line of track, twisting
into the insubstantial,
already-foreign landscape,
the freight train's whistle
resembles a question
dying away in silence.

Posthumous

Reduced to its transience,
body and spirit,
cloud that disembodies itself,
wafting breath and foliage.

A charmed element,
once the fire within the fields,
distant warmth, promise
in the flaming circle of twilight, legend,
the smoldering glow's heart of night.

The ashes yellow-gray,
their foul smell
doesn't escape the urn.
Sink her in the garden,
not too far away;
the one I was
would like to remain with you.
The ancients honored
ash and dust.

Understanding

To read the letter in the letter,
to speak with him of
the unspeakable.

Desire has its seasons,
beauty withers,
words will be forgotten,
writing obliterates.

To love each other—those
who haven't lost us
in the already-thickening fog
of their and our lives.

It's not properties that bind;
that late nearness grants
what, attested neither in writing nor orally,
is effectible, but not destructible,
recognized by each other at first sight.

It wasn't the meaning of the words,
it was the voice,
the tone, the oscillation,
an incidental gesture—
clung on after the first farewell,
a wide-open silence
sealed under the lid.

White Rosebud

White agglomeration in timeless night,
pre-creation emptiness, world of the primordial bud,
before a foreign will burst it open;
time and matter arose in the origin.
We know little. Prevailed, clamored,
tricked a demon? Did nature create herself
out of herself,
flung what streamed and awaited her incarnation
by transformation through spheres
that unfolded themselves, bloomed, wilted
under the breath of the god,
and bloomed into new stars?
Cosmic rose, incarnation as small as a heart,
when we dive
after love and meaning.

Looking Back

All the trains have departed.
Standing here, my gaze follows the flock of birds,
I sense eyes in the sky,
an ardent draft
as it preoccupied us in those tumultuous years.

Over the threshold
you arrive not unharmed.
To eradicate character,
machines and their words
amputate
children's attempts at speaking.

With early words and obstinacy,
I persuade myself,
infiltrate, skim through
the border: messages
between magnetic fields
spread through time.

Forest Cemetery (after Mörike)

For Martin Bircher

Walking in the infant forest,
the young fir trees. How they stand
so fresh and green,
so firm and bold.
In friendship, they stir toward us
their still-sparse, delicate treetops—
soon they will overshadow us,
each fir
guarding a grave.

Estrangement

Let us leave things
as they are,
let us not coerce them into the word.
Words are like wind,
the thing remains itself,
survives us—up close,
indescribable and distant,
the trickling of ashes and a black star
in your trembling hand.

Question and Complaint

Those who remained with us,
those who left us?
Question and complaint.
Some experience only their own suffering.

Many-faced truth
whispers and calls through time,
when it opens itself to eyes,
to landscapes, dreams; —writing
transforming back into signs;
you understand when what they indicated
has passed.

After Anesthesia, November 11, 2005

Last leaves in sight,
she goes astray in her own house,
believes she's still in the hospital,
steps through the bedroom door
into M's infirmary waiting room.

Outside, in the distance,
three cows in the mist,
the sparse autumn grass, the forest silhouette;
in front of the window, the empty tree.

In two houses diabolically wedged
into one dwelling,
she commits words and names to memory
behind which nothing comes to light.
Their meaning
has to be searched for like a needle
in the twilight: on the ground, a spark
that flashes, extinguishes
under grabbing hands, probing fingers.

Out of the house of cards,
my boundless bewilderment,
I stare at three cows.
Still I can count them;
still I can see the disrobed tree,
the skeleton, its beautiful winter form,
November bride shrouded in mist;
I see it in the soft dress and the crown of blooms
of a very distant bygone
spring arriving—
and, to my irritation,
in a no-longer-
not-yet-measurable time.

The Cold Night

After a night without stars,
I wait
for the coming light
at the end of the tunnel, the glow
without which we cannot survive;
we, the deluded,
self-delusional
out of the will to live—
unwilling to descend
into that mountain,
the self-consummating
death in darkness.

Directions

Don't look down,
step away from the chasm,
go into the land,
go inward,
toward yourself.

But who is that? I?
A heart filled with life
separated by counted breaths
from a nothingness
that was once everything.
I loved to live.

The Stillness

> *Reminiscent of a night-long
> demonic storm on Lake Garda*

After the hurricane
—the wailing of the sirens,
chaotic dissonance—
in the early blue,
a stillness over the water.

An intuitive stillness moves from eye to eye
between old ones who
still love each other.
That throbbing stillness
behind words,
heartbeat-stillness. We eavesdrop
on blood and hearing. You and I,
speechless dialogue, reprieved.

Snowfall-stillness,
when the restlessly baffled
dream the dream of God.

Stillness over the sites,
absolute and indefinite,
voices no one hears anymore.

Cast Out
(Desert)

With God cast out
do humans remain alone
like a puddle, an animal,
a sign scratched
on a sunken stone?

What do pious atheists
think, feel,
when with a wordless prayer in their heads,
they seek consolation in the knowledge
that the astronomical God
has no finite end,
and boundlessness remains
unresponsive?

The Legendary Shepherds

For Maria

They saw nothing yet, but heard
singing as far as the spheres, and listened
dumbstruck and wide-eyed
as an unknown red
burned itself through night's cloud formations.
It flooded and climbed and blazed—
then they ran, not comprehending,
and proclaimed
a new humanity,
and a light effused
over deserts, valleys, heights, beyond time.
Later it was said the shepherds
saw the heavens open—
angels with the animals,
and painfully close,
a tail-trailing star.

Sheep in the Snow

Weather-grey, a low fog:
seventeen sheep
under the lackluster light,
in pairs, threesomes, alone;
scrabbling, plucking, yielding
their streaky glances, askew,
a hungry bevy
of dull white herd animals.

When they recognize
the large flake in the dense snowfall
up there on the path,
they bear down on me
across the slanted wide pasture,
jostling upslope, clumped
into a single churlish fleece,
craving head to head, jerking,
shying back
from the electric fence, ogling,
shoving and pushing, waiting,
scrunch shriveled apples
with grinding mouths
in the old snow
marked by their hooves.

The bleating of a lamb
in the frosty night
cannot be located—
it complains for us all—
its track through time,
our blood in the snow, stillness and complaint,
the long night
and short days.

Evening

Under day-weary eyes, hands
that do nothing,
settle down into the evening;
when a weak wind shifts clouds
the grass doesn't sense it,
a blade perceives it,
shimmers and bobs,
gives encrypted signals
to an extinguished land.

A bird switches the tree,
that spot of down
under the wings flashes—
a late ray of light is a promise
and a swan a figure of thought
when it bends over the water—
depth as a game of light. Dusk falls.

To live with
the fading, the blackening
of the blue on the eastern mountain;
to find where one wasn't looking,
wordless happiness, speechless suffering
against which words are shattered—
two nights ago, my death-dream.

Quickly the young moon sinks in the west,
is fruit, word and scythe:
symbol of the new beginning of a world
that submerges when we go.

Gras (*Grass*)

The box where
the croquet equipment was stored,
reminded me
of an animal or a child's coffin.
It terrified me, that prismatic box,
with its massive metal carry-handles,
its wooden mallets,
rusty arcs.

Sarg, the German word for coffin,
written backward, is *Gras*.
... Grass grew over the coffin.
After the fire, it's better
to rest in an urn
that might hold oil, wine
or wheat, instead of ashes—
substances that nourish life,
whose joy was grass—
in my sad childhood
sheltered by the flowers' eyes.

The Shadow

When your shadow
has become figurative—
as one who separated himself from you—
you shouldn't follow him,
don't follow him, let him go,
even when he looks back,
waves like a lover—
remain steadfast in your body,
turn away,
mensch, fool of your hope,
believing to be of another nature—
child of a god
in a hundred,
in no incarnation,
who doesn't want to be recognized.
When he breathes on you, the breeze
can't be warded off.

Morning Twilight

Between dull panes,
the torn web slack,
the spider gone,
the booty spoiled.

The birch in the window tousled by the wind,
headache-wind, branches like hair:
swaying, beseeching on the spot.

With the birch in view,
I practice my loneliness,
a broken branch
given up by its tree
who counts its years and days.
It must dance alone
in the grip and breath of the wind;
it dances, no longer ensouled.

The Bridge

Wobbly and high up,
that gangplank to the other bank,
without railings,
with gaps and holes
in its slippery boards.
Don't look down; down there
the current marks the border, rushing on forever.
Look directly ahead to the grove
of white flowers and black cypresses;
walk the moon-path,
the snowy paleness,
always straight ahead and alone
into the nameless oblivion
when twilight flows from the mountain
out of blue goblets
where we drank
the water of life.

2

The Message in the Snowflake

Path

Walking alone and as a couple,
not overlooking the omens,
and in clear view,
the dial-less clock.

Childhood in the Old House

In the bleak garden, the house is a tower,
and within, eight stairs from earth's depths
all the way under the arch of the pitched roof.
In the stairwell, the central wing, back and forth,
Father's tread and voice, Father
speaks to himself, foreboding dark things,
hammers, nails doors shut.
Above, seventeen steps away,
the child cowers on the stairs while Mother and Sister
are listening, hoping
the drunken hunter has forgotten
his wife and children in the forest.

Nightmares flow
into lead-heavy sleep at three in the morning.
The morning is sallow early,
a tattered sky hangs within the window's sash bars.
Yet the pigeon coos in the ivy,
and behind the flowering blackthorn,
scurrying birds small as children's fists
reluctantly opening
in front of downy buds.

This, the risen father knows,
is the second-to-last ice age—
"The spring, children, begins
when in May cold pellets
snow on buds and bird's nests."

Elective Affinity

For Ernst

You are what I am not,
I am what you are not,
our natures don't coincide;
still, we love each other,
recognize glances,
clasp each other's hands;
you are me, I am you;
we stand up
to death's servants,
those defilers of the soil
and weavers of golden nets.

We are both
astounded by flowers,
creations of the spirit, of kindness,
puzzles of space and time,
admire life-and-death courage,
live from our own roots
in elective affinity
with the other's foreign images
reconciled in patience and love.

When you walk in the charmed forest
and the universal time of your childhood
that opened up early, a dreamer and doer,
I sit at the window, stuff holes,
lose myself in memories
of loved ones and the dead,
in red heaths and white nights—
rediscover myself
in your latest book.

Dark Hour

Scanning the extinguished horizon
for images nurtured, lapsed long ago,
I see you propped on Father's pitchfork
that stoked, jabbed and dug,
mucking the topsoil with ashes—
see you brooding in the autumn fire
as if you had glimpsed something unspeakable
in the burning bush or saw the sparkling lily
of the garden fountain
rising and falling
until the wall's shadow blackens it,
and inch by inch, plants
and human silhouettes
become one.

Not every image has its inner incarnation.
Its inner-world honesty
awash in exhaustion,
when tears drench the eyes
in the dark.

Pre-Pre-Spring

In the afternoon I collect kindling,
make out lumps
on naked bark,
tiny pustules,
dots of hope,
and the arctic air
hits me square on.

At night I skirt the trees
webbed in the late moon,
the mirror of ice-light that seals the pond;
far above in the cold constellations
I search out my deceased,
before a sinister fish
swallows the satellite,
and a gust scatters
the souls.

Alley

In our crabapple alley
interspersed with crooked, mossy
pear trees,
magnolias, wild cherries, quinces—
I dive into the deep-time of fragrance and flavor
of mythical apples with names
like *Jonathan, Reinette*—
and find light-green, shiny-matte,
crisp apples. You stooped
toward them in the dewy morning grass,
paused in the middle of the path,
bent over the fruit, an artifact,
sniffed it
with flared nostrils
like an apple
with a paradisiacal origin.
Had it not always been the first,
without blemish?
A child's apple, an apple-child
early in August.

At five this morning
a lightning storm split and felled the old one.
Unlike any other, in its hollows it offered
complete protection to bird's nests,
and when one walked by, cheeping and clamor
pined for nourishment—the chattering tree distracted
the sharp-eyed cat.

Old trees too,
are grateful for tenderness:
with the touch of my wrinkled hand,
the rough branches, the mossy-furred trunk
remind themselves
of pink blooms and summer apples
in years
no longer to be numbered.

Magical Number

A lad
surprises me while I'm playing:
"Gal!
If only you were 1000 weeks old!"
In her head, the child
divided 1000 by 50,
and arrived at a rounded-up cycle
of 20 years.
I considered the number, the cipher—
kept a guilty conscience because of those stolen
twenty-times-two weeks.

4420 weeks: my age.
A beautiful number but it doesn't appeal.
No magic will help
either orally or in writing,
even with the calculator.
I have to bear it, this 85 x 52
long-short time, a heavy,
a tedious burden no one will relieve me of—
nor give me 1000 weeks
of anticipation and happiness as fragile
as a June moth in late autumn.

Too young for the aged,
too old for the young,
I'm alone in the fear
that I might be discovered
by that night hunter, death.

Night Bird

How uneasy I feel
when the night bird calls—
its cry reaches far;
it's the welcome
in the sallow rays
of the other world,
when what you were and are—
a stone fallen out of its fittings
sinks through
its fate—
through all your layers
into non-being.

The Guest

Never again, "a foreign feeling
when the silent
candle glows"—
everything,
of course, is
strangely familiar,
closes in on me
with paws and grimaces;
and when the candle flickers late,
she stands in the draft,
Nemo didn't shut the door,
left it open
a crack—a guest
who remained so definitively silent
that an echo still clung on:
I'll return again,
is what I thought I understood,
my name stands
for permanence and peace.

The Coffin

Leaf-, root- and fruitless
it rots in the earth; disposed of,
a crate that pretends
to protect a larva.

The legend of the creature that flew out
was recounted to the child,
and she saw that little soul—
arms spread wide
like a dragonfly in steep flight
entering into the sky's
twilight—a blindness
that makes me
so uneasy today.

Sea of Fog,
as seen from Lindenberg

As far as the view stretches, a sea
surging in spheres of cloud,
tide and flow over the land, uphill,
the cliff stands proud, stands on the sea.

Down there we toil, scrape a living
in kitchens, warehouses, on fields,
at the bottom of the sea we cross streets,
have goals, build honeycombs,
are confined—and held back
by activities—,
neglect people, encounter animals,
return home under roofs,
eat, are sick;
blind to what is close, we watch television,
fall into sleep, waft in dreams
with closed feet, go astray
in shadowy gorges and paradises.

Ahead of me the frieze
of mountains rising out of the sea.
I'd like to walk on water,
should you come toward me from over there,
you whom I loved
in my other life
gathered in stillness.

White Death

Gapes in the window,
grimaces with black teeth, rolls white eyes,
doesn't move a limb, is void of feeling,
is a wild tangle
of gauzy scrub and gloomy stalks,
motionlessly gropes,
loses itself in fog, perseveres,
strangles me with knobbed fingers.
There were once elves,
their whispers and eavesdropping, that writing
of astral hieroglyphs, the sniggering
of the little Irish folk. He who saw them knows,
because as a child with dream-senses,
he was entertained by nymphs
as in a mirror
becoming cloudy; and late,
when Eros and Pleasure are off and away,
opening
on the earliest pictures and the last emptiness.
There's no soul there, if you're alone
with your graphically congealing nature,
with bodies, lines, foreign spaces,
masks on walls
in the snow-packed boughs.

There *is* a soul: the indigenous crow,
God knows what she picks from the rough
straggly fur that becomes more ragged
from night to night—
the crow, allowing herself to be seen,
suddenly clears off,
but will return, you hope,
the soul—.

For Markus Manfred Jung

Crow-stories and raven-tales,
scar and wisdom, mythical hour,
timeless memory and future tidings
in birdflight and last suns,
farewell-nights and open days.

Fatigue in March

Ice-cold feet, jittery hands
and the tip of the nose so mask-white
I see myself
like Faithful Henry in the fairy tales
who petrifies from head to toe,
muscle upon muscle.
I already stand half in the grave,
just about protrude,
with heart and face
in the light.

At once the flight of crows
streams above me
black as tatters of night,
and the adorable tomtits claw
themselves into the needles,
picking away, playing head-down.

The jays are there too,
spreading their little blue wings,
they reassure my eyes;
when in the old snow
that lost red glove appears to be
in the middle of the just-about-
recognizable world.

Waiting Room: The Protest

Beautiful visitor at the window: the small boy
stands nestled behind her
crossed legs. Mummy comments on pictures
in a travel magazine for doctors.
Hose or flaky branch?
Something green devours something white;
two wriggling legs dangle
out of the reptile's mouth, the boy
frowns: *What is that?*
A snake. She's eating a frog—
No she can't.
Mummy can't eat her child.
The mother: *È la natura.* She turns the page;
the boy stares a hole in the air,
takes possession of the magazine,
flips back,

no, he insists, *no no no no.*
The lips tremble. *No.*

In the door crack a white apron:
Mrs. S. with Francesco!
Pulled by Mother's hand,
he stumbles out of hell.

Forgotten Path

Westward.
Only still visible in the evening
when shine and shadow
fall more silently,
silver grasses and bloom-dust.
Once again a painful uprooting.

Evening path.
Those who walked here, where are they?
Some remained on this stretch,
many are dead. I see them,
see them walking. Each alone.
He walks, she walks
from wayside shrine to wayside shrine,
down from the moraine,
following the sun.
The white, the gray path is now green.
Like water on the deep grass, the glowing
of the earth's edges
falls over the valley in a fan of rays.

He who showed himself in the hour of the crickets
dives back into the earth,
carries his dead after midnight;
no one knows
where from and where to.

Harvest

Soaring clouds
over the fields:
in such a fashion the mountain is created,
and thus too mountain ranges disintegrate.
The thresher mows
until midnight
in that golden grain
that I've heard you could
vanish into
as into quicksand.

Hold on to yourself, spirit;
remember, soul:
the worlds are outside,
the land is inside.

Summer Solstice

Waiting at the window and staring outside
two mountains in the distant vapor
become a twin volcano.
The sun stands quite still
before it sinks.

Seeing what doesn't see us.
Constellations are of another nature.
Lucid moments: human glances.
They burn through water
before they extinguish.

Childhood Sun

Sun that sank—
and under the earth,
sailed over an ocean
to the morning mountain.

How long the day is in August
when the crows
invade the dazzling
stubble-field.

Devouring the sky,
the day-star swells;
when the forests are sealed off,
it becomes lost in a white glow.

Behind trees
the sun finds itself again,
its loneliness when birds
and cloud-messengers leave it alone:
razor-sharp, concentrated and already distant,
the forest's edge still shimmers
in clusters of silver-washed butterflies,
large, matte,
that lost their gold dust.

Among wild marjoram and thistles, the child
pupates in the light, an ancient blue;
are they here? true to place and hour,
thistles and child,
turning blue in the inner vision?

About Waking from Dreams

Back from the country
that can't be found on any map,
you're three heartbeats short,
warmed through and enlightened—
until the dream-skin bursts
and lightning flashes in the naked eye;
forcefully exposed, you reappear,
cast off by the blue bird.

Indescribable, the effort
to rid yourself of a bad dream,
to rediscover yourself again
after fighting in the land of death
where no one stands beside us
because God, gods and animals
have been driven away.

In order to wake up completely, we stand up—
make sure we are walking tall—
testing the earth's burden.

Night-Thought

In the night, the thought
of an hour so united with itself,
like the world without time
before the spirit released it.

In order to find it, we must
pass through the body.

Even though we know,
don't know,
hope opens itself
under a stony cloud.

Moon in March

Two sickles are still missing.
Oblong: an egg—you dazzle
dead stone, wake up fear, infect
with fevered light, confuse the brain,
extract my hysterical cry—
to be a helpless human being
like you who doesn't manage to evade
its phases.

Mock-bloom, blood-young leaves
in the winter boughs: the devouring frost and the vague hope,
when, with burning eyes
the ghost in the nightshirt
stares up to the light-blanked no-man's-sky
of our contaminated sphere.

Reading Material

Books on boards, on shelves!
Books layered in leaning towers,
spread across the floor of the room.
Who reads that? reads it a second, a third time?
Who disposes of the clutter
of human work and drudgery?

Knowing that books and their authors
vanish right down to a few annotations and names,
I'd prefer flowers, even pictures
of distant oceans and closer moors,
and in the window the flight
of a meteor.

*"If Nature didn't know how to contract and consolidate
the smallest and, for us, wholly unrecognizable, how
might she start to satisfy her human needs?"*

Goethe to Chancellor von Müller, found
in a dog-eared volume.

Silent as tree-breath, the word survives,
respires in darkness and stillness;
night-reading-material: the pain and the enchantment,
last love of the lonely.

Glancing at the healthy and the sick bindings,
I wouldn't sacrifice a single one.

From the Cloud Nation

Who lie in the sky,
whose profiles can be read
as stories without words,
now clear as a line, then blurred
as random strokes of writing, fleetingly noted,
they soar, they fly;
I observe them
as if addressed by a people
from bygone years with a steep incline—
animals too from another earthly age.
They lie, rest reclined, they soar,
a head without a body, drift
dreamlessly apathetic—
I watch them, forget them,
before they dissolve, transform,
blow away over a landscape
already foreign to me,
those nameless ones
from the cloud nation.

Vita

I have become my own foreign body,
remember that I was once
one with my vision and hearing,
with speech and walking.

Early morning twilight. I freeze, I heat up.
My hands are sooty.
Temper and hair dusty.
How it scatters, the yellow, the white ash,
how quickly—poured through the grating
and shoveled out—the sparks burn up.

In the window, as if it still existed,
that old *Robinia* tree,
a lord in its old age,
bony and bald;
the crows' throne before they
flew in relays over winter fields
and fog-steamed clods.

Roosters! Mörike! don't crow anymore,
but I have to light the fire
until the forest ranger sends the hunter
to collect me
for the greater brood.

Mid-Winter Spring

Out of the dented, rising moon
it's snowing light;
from the dark room;
standing at the window, I look downslope
toward fields of moonlight, the light-gray roofs.
How heavy they press
on sleepless old people.—As a child
I could fly in my dreams.

Not a soul anywhere. Stones and stillness.
The road white under the mock-mild light.
Frozen and jittery, I don't trust the devious game
of this January spring.
With my forehead on the naked-cold windowpane,
shuddering, I feel the wind
that drew long foehn-fishes through midday—
I'm worried about the snowdrop buds.
I sense the cyclamen scattered in the moon-snow,
children of fire and ice on Mount Etna.

I eavesdrop—
hear the sleeping angel crackling,
greet the sparse late-night stars,
search for the tracks of air, remember the footsteps
of loved dead ones,
count heartbeats, count years.

Stones and stillness.
The moon's reach across the valley
I'd once soared over—
that no one may set foot upon.

Getting Dark

Toward six-thirty p.m. the fields are extinguishing,
the forest is swallowed up in the twilight
of the lowlands—
when the sky revels, the world is unbounded,
the heights crystalline,
the silhouette of the mountain forest, pitch-black.

Flamingo-red.
Cranes stretch their long necks,
struggle toward night;
since in the tree-crowns light fades,
its last ray
breaks on the threshold of the roots,
voices become loud, voices fall silent,
the eyes in the knot frighten, are frightened.

As darkness thickens, contours sharpen
and the bodies are rubbed out.
When shadow upon shadow nod to each other,
when the forest grows over the land,
grows over the creek, the bridge, and the child,
when the wind whispers with leafy tongues,
leaves the tree-gate
open for a long time, the birds sleep,
the bark-gullies crawl with vermin
searching the afterglow

of stars extinguished long ago—
more distant than a world.
Forest—primeval age. Its language,
a hush that defies translation.

Key Word

For Silvia Haab

Between waking and sleep
considering words,
under closed lids
eyes are insightful.
There are words
that have a heart, recall faces,
protect places, spaces and time.

The word,
comprehensive and clear,
finds you; stop looking
and the secret word is recognized,
leads you—
lost in death,
timelessly trusted in a dream—
a warm, pulsing,
tender hand.

Death and the Woman

For Ernst

I roamed through the fields,
picked flowers, collected names,
winters went and springs came,
and with them, guests; I liked those
who read books and wrote letters.
I love people who love.

Nothing has remained.
Today my joy is a painless hour,
the absence of that circle
of grim ghouls without countenance.

Master!
Do not touch me.
The light still reaches me,
I am still able to complain,
to question the stillness,
to comprehend what rings on; I wake up
in shock in lost places—
I am still permitted to make words
out of my lost
naked face.

Spring

In the field in the morning
an Abel-fire burns,
Cain lost
and God in the garden.
New earth begins.

The Message in the Snowflake

Pentecost morning.
Over the hedge
the sunlit flight of a snowflake.

Spirit that drifts where it wills
bloom that carries off
seeds that plant feet.

The root reaches deep,
the one I tread upon—
in my eyes, the flake
vanishing in the light.

ERIKA BURKART:
Fragments, Shards, and Visions

Swiss poet Erika Burkart (1922–2010) has been compared to the likes of Ingeborg Bachmann, Friedericke Mayröcker, and Rainer Maria Rilke. During the latter half of her lifetime, the Swiss literary establishment perceived her not only as the *grande dame* of Swiss-German poetry, but also as an elusive, metaphysical, at times eccentric enigma of contemporary German-language literature.

Born in Aarau, Switzerland, Burkart published over 24 collections of poetry and nine prose works, writing for the most part in the house of her childhood (the former summer residence of the Prince-bishop of Muri), Haus Kapf in Althäusen, Aargau, which was run as a tavern by Erika's parents.

Burkart received numerous literary prizes during her lifetime, including the Conrad-Ferdinand-Meyer-Preis (1961) and the Gottfried-Keller-Preis (1992). To date, she is the only woman ever to have been awarded Switzerland's highest literary prize, the Grosser Schiller (2005). Friedrich Dürrenmatt and Max Frisch were also recipients of this prize (1960 and 1973 respectively).

When I first informed a member of the Swiss literary community that I was planning to translate Erika Burkart into English, there was a pause of silence followed by a wry smile. "Ah, the fay, the sprite, the fairy poet," she said. Over the years, film and photo footage of Erika in her family home and garden show her as a wistful, light-spoken woman in flowing dresses with daisies woven in her hair—a veritable child of nature. On this subject, Ernst Halter, Burkart's husband and literary partner for more than 40 years, tells me, "This was a myth that grew out of public misunderstanding that lasted for most of the time we were together. The myth had several sources: a few early poems, her delicate and soft-spoken personality, her strong connection with nature, and above all else her dresses! There are literally closets and closets full of them and she designed most of them herself." Pirmin Meier, author and contemporary of Burkart's, once noted: "Erika Burkart was not the nymph from Haus Kapf in Murimoos—where she lived most of her life—she was an observer and rational thinker with an extraordinary depth of vision."

Burkart's poems often begin with tactile images of nature in Haus Kapf's flowering garden (which she adored), the view across the moor and into a distance of gently rolling hills. The landscape, the seasons, the temperamental weather, the flourishing flora and fauna of this corner of Aargau feature in much of her verse. At first glance many of her poems appear to be concise and straightforward lyrical testaments to the natural world—yet, behind her trees, birds, snowflakes, and flowers, there is something far-reaching and transcendental at work. Oft-recurring protagonists include the cloud, the flake, and the tree. The cloud in particular is an important motif in Burkart's writing, a symbol of transformation or metamorphosis. In her poem "Reden und Schweigen" from *Geheimbrief*, 2009 ("Speak and Hush" from *Secret Letter*), the last book she saw published in her lifetime, she compares her thoughts to migrating, ever-transforming, churning clouds:

> *Lonely talk, written,*
> *conversations with the dead; thought-conversations,*
> *thoughts like clouds churning,*
> *black birds out of thin air,*
> *the white dove out of a dark cave.*

Perhaps, as Pirmin Meier has suggested, "...with her word-magic she was attempting to repair that broken thread between man and nature. (...) I see in her poetry a late attempt—possibly in the last hour—within a world of suffering, brutality, aggression, and destruction, to read nature's signatures with awe and admiration." There is another "broken thread" that appears repeatedly in Burkart's writing, however, and it may well constitute the source of her approach to natural imagery: namely the unbridgeable divide between human perception and language's ability to convey it in its entirety. Erika's poems are compelling in their evocative language and their imagery, not only as testaments to the subtle power of nature, but also to the way that sensory information "approaches" elucidation. At times there is a sense that the poet is mistrustful, almost regretting the use of "human" words to approximate the glory of nature—and yet, there is also an acknowledgment that there are few ways available to capture some part of what will soon be lost. Over and over, Burkart demonstrates how language, thought, and that fleeting moment of observation are all one aspect of the natural process and are inextricably intertwined. An example of this poem-as-process is a personal favorite from the collection *Geheimbrief*, 2009 (*Secret Letter*), "Vogel. Ein Dank" ("Bird. A Thanks"). Here is the last stanza:

> *I let you take my soul*
> *as you swooped by the window,*
> *Bird, thought*
> *that writes with feathers in the sky,*
> *that wavers on wings,*
> *luster and shadow,*
> *sketching and measuring in flight,*
> *a word that evades me.*

The image of a bird drawing a word in the sky—a word the poet is trying to locate but cannot—suggests that Burkart regarded the natural world itself as a language, a compendium of phenomena consisting of interwoven patterns whose structure and sense is "legible" to us in varying degrees. In a linguistic sense, her poems correspond to a process of converting fleeting impressions into words. Yet the inverse of this idea is equally applicable in this context: the notion that language itself is a natural process among processes, and thus subject to the same set of principles. Burkart seemed to be searching for a golden mean between the word and the interconnectedness of all things—between nature, the cosmos, and human history; between the passage of time, the finiteness of life, and the phenomenology of human perception. Her quest was to define and locate her existence in the universe through poetry.

As Ernst has informed me, Burkart never defended her work against critics: "She was, in fact, entirely disinterested in what they thought about her; she was even mostly disinterested in her audience." Burkart lived for her poetry; so much so, in fact, that a number of her contemporaries have said they believe the only reason she managed to live to the ripe age of 88 (she'd had a heart condition all her life) was because she never stopped pushing the boundaries of her unique and subtle form of verse. One might say that through her poetry (and a lifelong endeavor to reinvent and hone her craft and ideas), she sought to illuminate a metaphysical connection between the duality of life and energy, of the inner and outer nature of things; of how fragments and shards (fleeting snatches of memory, of images, of myths and legends) expressed through the imprecise medium of words are the only clues we have to puzzle together a semblance of what the world is / may be.

A critic once asked her why she wrote. "Why do you breathe?" she asked him in return. To Erika Burkart, writing poetry was the breath of life.

* * *

What follows is a Sunday conversation with Ernst Halter at Haus Kapf over tea, cake, and the occasional jigger of malt whiskey. While Burkart was still alive, she and Ernst had made their "tea hour" a period of daily reflection and meditation. It was a time of the day they would catch up on each other's projects and discuss anything of interest. As I enjoy this "tea hour" with Ernst, Burkart's writing desk sits to my left, in the corner of my eye.

MV: *Had you heard of Erika before the two of you met? How did you meet?*

EH: I had read some of her work, but had no idea she was living here in this particular house. I had come to Haus Kapf because I had heard that there were these very old and fascinating frescos on the walls. On that Friday evening on the 23rd of June 1967, I walked up the steps, and there she was standing at the top looking down. I was astonished. We walked up together and she showed me the frescos. We talked for two hours that seemed like two minutes—and that was it: we both knew that we had found our soul mate.

MV: *Erika was never really interested in living abroad then? She loved to be at home here in the house of her birth?*

EH: Early on she had lived for about six months in Milan, but she never got along with the city. For one thing she had an awful sense of direction. She once told me the only way she could navigate around Milan was to try and recall landmarks—she had no idea about roads or avenues, she simply couldn't figure these things out in her head. She was in her element here, overlooking the moor.

MV: So how and where do you see Erika's place in German-language literature?

EH: As a lyrical poet of the post-war period, writing over sixty years, her place in German-language poetry is utterly unique. In my opinion, there is no other poet writing in German during that period with a similar development. Her many publications stretch from 1953 through 2011, and through all those years, from book to book—up until the very last day—her work went through phenomenal transformations.

MV: We both know that Erika's mythos in Switzerland is mostly of a soft-spoken, shall we say, metaphysical or hermetic nature poet. What is it that makes Erika's poetry unique?

EH: The uniqueness of Erika's poetry is based on a "lived and innate" conviction of the process of metamorphosis—the relationship, even the "parentage" of every organic and inorganic creature, plant, or substance. What is separated on the surface can be perceived and understood as being one with its roots; a kind of metamorphosis *à rebours* (lived backwards). Here's a passage from her notes:

> *To recognize something one has to look with both the material and the spiritual eye at the same time. One helps to see the other; the image forms when looking. In order to understand what you see, you require a third eye.*

What she means is: her poems work (function in) "the metamorphic way" from the material (the body) moving in to the spiritual.

MV: And here's a quote from one of your essays, Ernst, regarding Erika's view of the duality of all things:

> *Here is there, there is here. Even eternity is encapsulated in time despite the fact that time is voided through eternity. What appears to be hidden is visible—what appears to be visible is hidden.*

Can you tell me how her interest in nature, cosmology, mythology may have influenced her work? There has been some talk of her being influenced by the writings of Paracelsus.

EH: More important for Erika were perception and grounded science—she wanted clarity. She was very well read in biology and later, physics and astronomy — which she studied from all periods of history. She was extremely curious.

MV: And her almost mythical belief in the power of the word?

EH: The "word" for Erika was her first instrument of perception (how she loved foreign words!), but she knew that "the word" is not the "final" thing. Here's a citation from her notes:

> *When studied in a certain infinitesimal detail, every word imbues meaning—(a reference tension)—concerning the "basso ostinato," the theme of a love melody. For that reason: the polyphonic character of our existence.*

MV: *What of Erika's perception of the place of the individual in the scheme of nature and the cosmos—the socio-critical element of Erika's work?*

EH: Erika's love of nature came about in her childhood. Basically, she could go where she wanted and do as she liked. Mother had no time. Father had no interest. Just outside her front door was Swiss nature at its purest. She really had a wonderful youth from that point of view. Her parents never told her she had to be back at a certain hour. They basically let her run wild. Erika was very critical of man's role in nature from the very beginning — in particular as far as her own immediate natural world was concerned, the ecology and environment that she had adopted as her "other" sibling, her ally.

MV: *What would you say was her most prolific period of political writing?*

EH: After 70. All through her work, starting with about the third published collection, there are political poems; but it's not outspoken politics, it's more like an insight into what occurs. There is, for example, one poem where she sees a man somewhere on a little road and she imagines what moves this man to be there, and what will come out of his actions. It's a political poem, but not outspokenly so.

From *Transparenz der Scherben*, 1973 (*The Transparency of Shards*), "Orientierung" ("Orientation"):

> *Traffic accident dead. War dead.*
> *Casualty coincidence crime.*
> *(It could just as easily*
> *have taken you or me):*
> *When I read the newspaper,*
> *those lovers of roses look suspicious.*
> *I'm a gardener with a guilty conscience.*
>
> *It seems difficult to deal with people who*
> *enjoy poetry,*
> *climb mountains,*
> *attend concerts,*
> *water radishes,*
> *who talk about rights, guilt and justice.*
>
> *I lose*
> *all sense of orientation.*
> *In place of words I see fists,*
> *gestures, faces, isolated faces.*

I see everyone alone with himself:
an almost harmless person,
just because he's sad or he's happy.

I fear the man whom nobody misses.
At a single blow he forces us
to picture him.
There's nothing yet
about this man in the newspaper.
One knows him on sight.
It's now too late to love him.
....
Every day
the Bridge of San Luis Rey collapses.
We're badly informed
because it tires us quickly —
in a burst to precisely follow
the flight of a single flake.

"Their manes flowed like a snowstorm,"
Black Elk said of the sacred horses.

Who killed the sacred horses?
The red? the black? the white men?
It has been said the grass grew over them.
— We
kill them now.

Invocation revocation obituary.
Men shrivel to names.
Names are words. Words flake.
Black flurry. Alphabet snow.

Holding on to the empty margins,
I hear
the growing
of grasses.

* * *

At the turn of the century, before a "relatively" sedentary life at Haus Kapf, Walter Burkart, Erika Burkart's father, had been a hunter and adventurer in the wilds of South America. He appears over and over again in Burkart's poetry and prose, mostly as a foreboding, sometimes terrifying figure. Even in Geheimbrief, 2009 (Secret Letter), Burkart's father makes an appearance. Here's an excerpt from the poem "Evening Parlor":

> ...we bring
> picture after picture into the winter parlor,
> now you can talk, now you're free
> from quarrels with Mother,
> now I'm free of my Father-fear.

EH: Walter Burkart was no Bruce Chatwin figure, no gentleman adventurer with a monocle and hardhat and a merry band of luggage-wielding natives. He was a tooth-and-nail, gun-toting, rough-and-ready survivor. Eventually he made his living hunting herons for their feathers in Argentina, but started out in Brazil panning for gold. For eighteen years he struggled in the wilderness of Brazil, Argentina, Paraguay, and Bolivia. It was a hard life, but he adored every minute of it. When he finally decided to get married and settle down here in rural Switzerland with Erika's mother, Marie Glaser (who until that time had been working as a governess in Ireland), he took up the bottle—and, let me tell you it was no avocation, it became his substitute bed-partner. He could have borne the risks of malaria, yellow fever, gangrene, leeches a thousand times over, but he couldn't tolerate life here in quiet, rural, *domestic Switzerland. He missed his pumas and caiman and howler monkeys and herons (and his Indio wives…). Ernst smiles. He shows me Burkart's father's cabinet of curios, a collection of stuffed Amazonian animals and bones, including a caiman skull and the largest armadillo I've ever seen.*

MV: *He published a book,* Der Reiherjäger vom Gran Chaco (The Heron Hunter of the Gran Chaco), *which became an instant bestseller.*

EH: Yes, just the one—it kept him occupied in the early years of the marriage; apparently, he wrote it from beginning to end with virtually no edits or corrections.

> *At first you still know what month it is, but soon you lose your bearings and you stop counting. Finally, you understand how the wild Indians feel, the fact that they don't know how old they are, and in fact, are even not familiar with the concept of time. Perhaps this is the reason that they are happy children of nature since there is no haste or stress in regards to tomorrow or the day after tomorrow.*

He writes somewhere in his book that whenever you had a wound in the jungle, you should quickly pour gunpowder over it and ignite it. You could see the scars on his hands. He had a very close relationship with the indigenous people and assumed the role of midwife innumerable times. He knew a little more about basic medicine than they did. He always said, never dabble with the local women, but Erika was firmly convinced she had some stepbrothers and stepsisters somewhere on the Grand Chaco.

MV: He never managed to settle into life back in Aargau?

EH: The locals were not interested in his fantastical adventures—who knows if they even believed him. Walter frequently swore to Erika's mother: "I'm going to sell. I'm going to sell." That's why Maria was always present in the tavern. With his signature he could have sold the house, but somehow she always managed to prevent it.

MV: How old was Erika when Walter's book came out?

EH: His book was released in 1934 or 1935, so Erika would have been around twelve. Walter was never a real father to Erika. She writes in her memoirs that he only gave her a gift three times in her life. Once it was a pack of VIP cigarettes, once an eggshell, and once it was his book. That was it, nothing for birthdays or Christmas. He just didn't care. Erika writes that she believed she was a lovechild. She was born just 12 months after Walter and Marie got married, her sister came two years later. It was only during the last years of his life that Walter finally became peaceful. He would lie in bed all day and reflect upon his former life. He used to say, "Ich gehe in die Jagdgründe." Which means he went back over there, back to his jungle. I regret I never had the chance to meet him. In me he would have found someone who would have been interested in his past. Possibly one of Erika's most poignant and direct poems about her father, "Mein Vater" ("My Father"), comes from the collection *Die Zärtlichkeit der Schatten*, 1991 (*The Tenderness of Shadows*):

> *A good hunter. An awful father.*
> *In death he went back west*
> *to the Indios whom he loved.*
> *His urn has a crack—*
> *now you're laughing, Father,*
> *you who never laughed;*
> *death was your friend—*
> *in his shadow*
> *we loved you.*
> *You always hit the mark, Father,*
> *us too,*
> *in our hearts.*

MV: *Did Walter have any literary influence on Erika?*

EH: Not directly—not really, other than appearing frequently in her works; but of course, his book was highly lauded in its time. In some strange way, Erika inherited his talent. Walter always said he never wrote about the most awful things. He simply couldn't write them—or perhaps he didn't want his family to know. Erika told me later that one of the most terrible things that happened to him over there was during Christmastime—and therefore, every Christmas, he was utterly intolerable. He never let on what had happened. A dark cloud cast its shadow over everything. Once in a while, when he was really drunk, he said he would shoot the whole family. Maria and the two girls would cower in one of these rooms with the doors locked. He'd stand in front of the door with his gun, and bark over and over: "Open, and I'll shoot you." These fears never left Erika; a demon lived in this house.

MV: A demon that had wrestled with crocodiles and panthers… And Maria, Erika's mother, was she interested in literature?

EH: Mother was the only place Erika could go. Maria was the first to appreciate her daughter's gift. Without Erika's knowledge she sent some of Erika's early poems to editors in Zurich. Brichner, a big literary figure of the time, recognized her talent immediately. He helped her publish her first small volume of poems in 1958, *Der Dunkle Vogel* (*The Dark Bird*).

MV: Of course, it was rhyming poetry.

EH: Yes, most of Erika's poetry was written in rhyme until the early eighties. In the beginning she wrote mostly nature poetry in the vein of Annette von Droste-Hülshoff, much later she moved on to free verse—though she never stopped rhyming completely, and she always had a strong sense of meter and cadence.

MV: And in those early days the family struggled financially?

EH: Erika's childhood was fraught with hardships and

poverty. It's one of the reasons she was forced to become a high-school teacher. She would have loved to get an advanced degree, but it simply wasn't possible. With her teaching job she managed to keep up the household for twelve years—and then suddenly, when she was about thirty years old, she had a heart attack. At this stage, her mother took up teaching again after having been out of that field for over twenty years. Every month they struggled to pay the bills.

MV: You've said before that although Erika couldn't make a living with her writing, she did eventually achieve notoriety.

EH: In the end—but actually it wasn't something she yearned for. All she really wanted to do was write. And although she was obliged to occasionally appear in public, she had great difficulties reading to an audience. Here's a short piece from her many unpublished notes and journal entries where she talks about it:

> *My voice sounded like it didn't belong to me. As soon as they were spoken out loud the words seemed foreign ... When the audience claps at the end, I stand here as if I've been scattered in ashes. I then stand off to one side and don't feel like talking to anyone.*

Erika had the broadest literary knowledge of anyone I've ever met. Our mutual appreciation of literature is really what drew us to each other and bound us together.

MV: So tell me about Erika the poet versus Erika the prose writer.

EH: Of course, Erika was more poet than prose writer, but she was well accomplished in both forms. When Erika wrote her first novel, *Moräne*, 1970 (*Moraine*), the general reaction in the press was: "Lo and behold, our great poet has written a novel." Later there was a reprint, and I wrote a foreword. The book is pure deconstructionism *avant la lettre* and it's the very best prose book she ever wrote, but nobody realized that at the time. Generally, Erika's prose is highly lyrical and imagistic, but she always struggled with getting the dialogue right.

MV: What was her process regarding moving between writing the two forms?

EH: If you are really immersed in a prose book, you normally don't write poetry. Your thoughts are completely absorbed in that novel you're writing—at least that's the way it was with the two of us.

MV: Was there a conscious decision to write a prose book?

EH: It wasn't a decision; it was a necessity. There was a deep-seated urge to write a novel or a collection of short stories. We spoke about this many times: while you continue on your daily regimen of writing poetry, the prose book or novel is building itself in an intensity. One day you can't stand it anymore, and you have to sit down and write "the

Book." I know it was precisely like that with Erika's novel *Die Vikarin*, 2006 (*The Lady Vicar*), and it was like that with my own last novel too. As soon as I'm sure I can write a book—and it was the same with Erika—it's like a boat trip on a lake at night and there are these buoys in the water somehow linking the novel together. The buoys are sentences or phrases. In the darkness I have to navigate from one buoy to the other. But I know precisely when I have reached the last buoy. Then I write straight through for six or seven months.

MV: And those buoys? Are they somehow sketched out on paper like a kind of map, so to speak?

EH: No, not at all. They're in my head, in my subconscious. And I know the precise sentence that must fall somewhere, and now I have to make the way to this sentence, and then I have to find my way to the next, which I already know precisely. So, in the end they turn out to be a kind of map, but not until the novel is complete. Very strange, I know.

MV: You've mentioned that you were convinced that Erika had "spiritualist" abilities.

EH: I'm firmly convinced that Erika was a medium, but she intensely disliked that idea. She frequently foresaw things that had not yet occurred, or she dreamed things that happened later. Erika's first husband, Yanosh, was an orchestra conductor. In her notes she actually prophesizes his death—but she would never have admitted it.

MV: Of course, many marriages with poets have tragic endings. Sylvia Plath and Ted Hughes come to mind.

EH: We were very lucky. When I think of Ted Hughes and Sylvia, it may be that those two were too close in their personality. Erika and I were quite different from each other; we had divergent interests. For example, Erika was a great botanist. I came more from physics and astronomy. Of course there were difficult times, and I had to have a strong personality to withstand when she went too far. Erika had many lovers, and they all left her sooner or later. None of them had the personality or patience or strength to withstand her tempers—she could be as terrifying as she was ravishing. I do believe my patience with her saved our marriage, and I firmly believe she was grateful to me for that. Many people prophesized that our marriage would end in disaster, but it worked perfectly.

MV: Did you know about Erika's illness from the beginning?

EH: Yes, I knew that Erika's heart was half the size of a normal heart. She was born like that, so she couldn't do much strenuous exercise, but she did still become 88 years old in spite of everything. Her health really started to decline seriously after 2000. She didn't want to die. She knew I would survive her—she was angry at me for that. The true farewell for me now has been the editing of her notes and memoirs. In the last years of her life (until she had to go to the clinic), she spent all the time in these two rooms, writing, resting, and looking out of these windows.

She could barely sleep and was in great pain. Writing her poetry was the only thing that kept her going. Many of the last poems were written in the early morning and late a night. Those years were awful. I always had the hope, when she was in the clinic (the morphine helped her recover slightly)... I always hoped I could take her back to the old house, but it was impossible...

MV: Erika wrote until she couldn't write anymore, until the words failed her.

* * *

In her very last posthumous poems, "Nachtschicht" ("Nightshift"), from the collection *Nachtschicht / Schattenzone*, 2011 (*Nightshift / An Area of Shadows*), in her battle against her loss of words (as Ernst explained to me), Erika once again reverted back to rhyme. Apparently this was the only fashion in which she could recall the words from her failing consciousness. In the second section of the book *An Area of Shadows*, fellow-poet Ernst Halter bids farewell to his companion and deepest friend for more than forty years. From *An Area of Shadows* by Ernst Halter, the poem "Your final thousand-and-first photo":

on a blister pack
with the tablets rustling inside
for the last of your nineteen weeks
in this hospice of the dying.
Two to be taken in the morning, one in the evening,
the window, Monday 7-9,
has broken through.
The telephone call when they asked where to let you die
came at three-thirty in the afternoon.

Terror and laughter contort your face,
imprecise, zero contrast, the eyes buttons,
even the red shawl,
your guardian and comfort: blur.
Pillows prop you,
in the right hand, a pencil twitches,
last weapon
for defense against such imposition.

A mug shot on room twozerofour,
so you wouldn't be confused
with an insane person.

Marc Vincenz
2013 | 2014

ERIKA BURKART was born in Aarau, Switzerland, in 1922. Throughout her career she published over 24 collections of poetry, 8 prose works, and was awarded numerous literary prizes, including the Conrad-Ferdinand-Meyer-Preis (1961) and the Gottfried-Keller-Preis (1992). She was the only woman ever to have been awarded Switzerland's highest literary prize, der Grosser Schillerpreis (2005). She passed away on April 14, 2010.

MARC VINCENZ is British-Swiss, was born in Hong Kong, and has published six collections of poetry: *The Propaganda Factory, or Speaking of Trees; Gods of a Ransacked Century; Mao's Mole; Behind the Wall at the Sugar Works* (a verse novel); *Additional Breathing Exercises* and *Beautiful Rush*. He is also the translator of numerous German-language poets, including Erika Burkart, Ernst Halter, Klaus Merz, Andreas Neeser, and Alexander Xaver Gwerder. Marc is the publisher and executive editor of *MadHat Press, MadHat Annual* (formerly *Mad Hatters' Review*) and *MadHat Lit*. He is Co-editor-in-Chief of *Fulcrum: An Anthology of Poetry and Aesthetics*, and serves on the editorial board of *Open Letters Monthly*. He is the founder of Evolution Arts, Inc., a non-profit organization that promotes independent presses and journals.

Other Books by Marc Vincenz

The Propaganda Factory, or Speaking of Trees
Gods of a Ransacked Century
Mao's Mole
Behind the Wall at the Sugar Works (a verse novel)
Beautiful Rush
Additional Breathing Exercises
(bilingual German-English selected poems)
This Wasted Land and Its Chymical Illuminations

Translations:

Kissing Nests (translations of Werner Lutz)
Nightshift / An Area of Shadows
(translations of Erika Burkart and Ernst Halter)
Grass Grows Inward (translations of Andreas Neeser)
Out of the Dust (translations of Klaus Merz)

www.ingramcontent.com/pod-product-compliance
Lightning Source LLC
Chambersburg PA
CBHW011613290426
44110CB00020BA/2583